"GROWTH DOESN'T HAVE TO COME FROM MORE.
IT CAN COME FROM LESS."

Simplicity
Entrepreneurship

Escape Burnout, Find Flow,
and Discover the Shortest Path to Profit

MILANA LESHINSKY

Published by:
Capucia, LLC
211 Pauline Drive #513
York, PA 17402
www.capuciapublishing.com

ISBN: 9781945252594
Library of Congress Control Number: 2019936402

Layout and typesetting: Ranilo Cabo

Printed in the United States of America

Simplicity Entrepreneurship

Escape Burnout, Find Flow,
and Discover the Shortest Path to Profit

To your
shortest & simplest
path to profit.

Milana

CONTENTS

What Is Simplicity Entrepreneurship and Why Should You Care?

Simplicity, simplicity, simplicity! I say, let your affairs be as two or three, and not a hundred or a thousand. Instead of a million, count half a dozen, and keep your accounts on your thumbnail.
—Henry David Thoreau, author, philosopher

You started your business with passion, excitement, and dreams of doing work you love. But now it seems as though instead of doing work that brings you ease and joy, you have a business that runs you and your life. You always feel like you have to be "on," and you have essentially traded one job for another.

It doesn't have to be that way.

You can go from feeling overwhelmed, drained, and frustrated to feeling confident, energized, and excited about your business again… and I can show you how. If you have been feeling confused, stressed, or burned out from trying to grow or scale your business, you're going to find relief and a solution in this short book.

Complexity is the enemy of profit. And right now there is available an overwhelming number of tools, strategies, systems, paths, mentors, and solutions for growing a business, which creates unprecedented complexity for entrepreneurs. Embracing simplicity can end the confusion, create results with more ease, and turn your vision into a highly lucrative business.

"Simplicity entrepreneurship" focuses on finding the shortest and simplest path to profit by identifying and avoiding everything that creates complexity. The goal is to eliminate unnecessary steps, tools, projects, activities, people, and mindsets that stand in the way of your company's growth. In other words, simplicity entrepreneurship is about designing a business around the path of least resistance, allowing you to grow it more organically.

Let's get started.

Who This Book Is For

When you clear the path to success –
that's when you consistently get there.
—*Gary Keller, co-author of* The One Thing

Although any entrepreneur can benefit from reading this book and applying the principles of simplicity entrepreneurship, it is primarily for life and business coaches, authors, speakers, experts, and information marketers who want to create highly profitable "lifestyle" businesses.

Growing a business online can be an exciting but overwhelming journey. Without having a way to discern the advice that's coming at you every day, you can find yourself confused and distracted. The strategies and mindsets in *Simplicity Entrepreneurship* will help you understand exactly what to pay attention to so you can create the lifestyle business you've always wanted. This is also for you if you're experiencing "business growth fatigue" and not sure how to untangle the complexity in your business. What I am about to share will reveal a much easier and more effective approach to growing a business.

Simplicity Entrepreneurship will challenge your thinking and beliefs about being an entrepreneur and transform your approach to business forever.

• • • • • •

THE SEVEN-FIGURE DREAM

Business is not a skill.
You don't get better by trying harder.
—Milana Leshinsky

When I imagined building a million-dollar business, I thought it would feel like a MILLION DOLLARS!

We measure the success of our businesses, consciously or unconsciously, when we hit a milestone like a six-figure or seven-figure mark, right? We feel like we achieved a certain level of success, impact, and status in our industry.

A seven-figure business is like the "Holy Grail" in online marketing. It's what we strive for. And we believe it's the ideal amount for a true lifestyle business. I was surrounded by people who were making seven and eight figures, so it became my goal, too. It felt like the only way to succeed or to be seen as a successful online entrepreneur was to reach that level of income.

But when I finally surpassed seven figures, I didn't even notice it. I was too busy working. It didn't feel like anything special happened – no more special than making six figures; no more special than getting a thirty-thousand-dollar job offer after college.

I was really confused and surprised by my reaction to finally having reached my biggest goal. It didn't make me feel any happier or more successful. Most important, I realized that my dreams did not match the reality of what I was living every day. I was always busy and stressed out, and even began having panic attacks, which were absolutely scary and debilitating.

So instead of celebrating the fact that I had made over a million dollars, I walked away from it all. I sold my business and went on sabbatical. In fact, the only thing I celebrated was the fact that I was able to let go of the idea that a seven-figure business meant success. Money alone just wasn't enough.

After leaving, I began to look closely at what was missing and to ask questions:

- *Was I crazy to walk away from a million-dollar company?*
- *Was my experience unique?*

- *And most important, where did I go wrong?*

I started my business back in 2001 when you could get an idea, create a website, and become a money-making pioneer in your niche. I remember sitting at my kitchen table in Carlisle, Pennsylvania, leading a teleseminar with people from Australia, Germany, Iceland, Canada. For many of them it was their first teleseminar ever! Everything was new and revolutionary. There were just a few ways to promote yourself online, and all you needed was the desire and drive. Life was simple.

If you were to start a business today, you would probably find yourself completely lost and overwhelmed with all the tools, skills, and strategies that you'd need to learn. Thousands of books, podcasts, programs, blogs, and mentors are ready to show you the ropes, each one firmly believing their method is the key to success, throwing you into a state of chaos, confusion, and, ultimately, burnout.

In fact, burnout seems to be the most common theme when I speak to seemingly successful business owners.

On the Brink of Burnout

*As in yoga, progress in business lies somewhere
between effort and ease. Do too little, and nothing
happens. Push too hard, and you'll burn out.*
—Milana Leshinsky

I recently surveyed thousands of coaches, authors, speakers, and entrepreneurs. Of those who responded, almost 92 percent said they were overwhelmed and stressed-out from the daily grind of growing their businesses. Some got really emotional and shared with me the fear, frustration, and pressure they felt to drive their businesses forward or to simply maintain what they had created. They felt like they had been thrown back into the same old rat race they had left when they walked away from corporate America. It was that feeling of being constantly "on" – selling, marketing, delivering, and thinking about their business 24/7.

Here are just a few things I heard:

- *"It's gotten so complicated. I just want to STOP."*
- *"Maybe I'm just not ready for this level of growth."*
- *"I hate to do this, but this is the way I have to do it to get the results I want."*
- *"I want to stop and walk away, but my clients need me and my team members rely on their income to take care of their families."*

…and here's a big one:

- *"People I thought were my role models are actually quite unhappy, so now I'm even more confused."*

As someone who had recently left a very successful seven-figure business myself, I began asking questions and digging deeper into what this is really about. In the process I made a fascinating discovery.

• • • ● • •

THE COMPLEXITY MINDSET

*Creating a simplified business that generates the
highest revenue possible doesn't mean not working.
It means working in ways that you love and
that suit you the best.*
—*Jonathan Fields, author of* How to Live a Good Life

Right now there's a shift happening in our industry. There have never been as many ways to spread your message and grow your business as there are today. You can scale and grow it any way you choose to, through social media, mobile apps, content marketing, video marketing, outsourcing, and collaboration. So we end up buying dozens of systems, investing in learning a lot of different skills, paying attention to hundreds of trends, and looking at each other to see what we should be doing. As a result, we find ourselves completely overwhelmed, confused, and drowning in the complexity we created. The problem is, we may not know we're trapped in complexity until something happens to make us take a step back and reevaluate our businesses and our lives.

The first business I created was very simple. My goals were simple. I was focused on staying home with my two small children and replacing my salary. Coming from a classical music background, I started completely from scratch. There weren't a lot of business coaches or experts to turn to back then, so I just did what felt natural to me at the time in creating and delivering products. I was even able to hibernate for a couple of months, enjoy lots of time off, and then do it all over again. In less than three years I was making six figures. In a few more years I was generating about half-a-million dollars a year working just five hours a day.

Then something changed. I was approached by another entrepreneur with an idea for a new business. I really liked the idea and we decided to partner. At the start everything was simple. We created an amazing offer, merged our connections, and enrolled over three hundred members into our new paid community. As a result, we generated over half-a-million dollars in the first few months.

Within a few years, as we tried to grow the business, it became too complex. We added dozens of events, launches, and programs and hired a big team that we had to manage. I began to put a lot of effort into our business, and for the first time ever I worked during my vacation. Even with all that hard work, however, our business wasn't growing. Our overhead was out of control and our revenue had plateaued, which began affecting our relationship.

Complexity killed our profit.

My friends noticed that I had changed. "Where's the Milana we know, the one who used to wake up excited about her business and couldn't wait to share her new ideas?"

Soon I got a clear sign that it was time to change something: panic attacks. When they first started, I had no idea what was happening to me. I'd never even heard of panic attacks before. I would just find myself suddenly dizzy, disoriented, or unable to breathe. I was scared and embarrassed because they were happening at any time for no apparent reason. When I started sharing this with other people, everyone offered a different opinion about why I was getting them. But one thing was clear: panic attacks were the messengers telling me that it was time to change something in my life.

I didn't yet know what it was I needed to change, but looking back now I can see that I had gotten caught up in the "complexity mindset." I dreaded about 70 percent of my work. I was doing things only because I saw others doing them. I was tackling the never-ending list of projects. I pushed myself hard, and when I didn't hit my income goals, I felt disappointed and confused. The complexity reached a point where I could no longer think clearly or enjoy my business.

What surprised me most, though, was that I didn't realize any of this until later. So you, too, might be operating on the complexity mindset right now and not know it. You might never get a panic attack like I did, but if you've been feeling stuck, overwhelmed, stressed out, or simply uninspired about your business, it's time to take a look at what might be causing it.

• • • ● • •

The Simplicity Principle

Simplicity is the key to building great wealth without succumbing to the pitfalls of inefficiency, complexity, and the resulting drain on your precious time and energy.
—Madeleine Davis, author, business strategist

Many business owners believe that growth has to come with stress, tradeoffs, or sacrifices. They hold back, worrying that if they were to start "playing bigger" and their business started growing, it might overwhelm or otherwise negatively impact their life. But there is a way to grow your business with peace of mind, clarity of direction, and confidence. I'm not saying it's easy; there are a lot of moving parts and skills you need to create any kind of growth. The good news is that it *can* be simple – if you understand the "simplicity principle."

The simplicity principle comes from Albert Einstein:

"Everything should be made as simple as possible, but no simpler."

This implies that less is more and that we should do only what's absolutely essential. Operating with the simplicity principle in mind means that you remove all the clutter and ignore all the "noise" in your business environment, revealing a beautiful, clear, and almost obvious path to growth.

So where does simplicity come from? In other words, what is simple? What is essential? How do you know what to keep and what to let go of or ignore? Here's the reality: Things are only complicated when we see them as complicated, so simplicity is subjective. What's simple to one person might be complex to another.

So instead of following what everyone else is doing or telling you to do, understand your unique personality and your natural abilities, then use them as guides to create a custom-fit business that is a full expression of you. **When you apply the simplicity principle you can let go of the clutter and experience a business that**

is so fully aligned with your personality that you're able to achieve optimal results with ease.

I'm about to show you how to apply simplicity to your business, but first let's get a few misperceptions out of the way:

- *Simplicity does not mean "simplistic" or "simple-minded."*
- *Simplicity does not mean you're scaling back, slowing down, or playing small.*
- *Simplicity does not mean you make less money.*

In fact, when you use the simplicity approach in your business, you can play as BIG as you want to. You can start a movement, achieve whatever goals you set for yourself – and do it without the struggle and frustration and without constantly measuring yourself against someone else. You can still push yourself and drive your business forward, but in the direction that is right for *you*.

When I first left my seven-figure business, I told myself, "That's okay. I don't need to play big. I'm okay having smaller goals." And I'll be honest, at the time that felt like the right place to be. But when

I discovered simplicity, I realized that you *can* play big as long as you make the simplicity approach your growth strategy. In fact, I got so excited about this whole idea and this new way to approach business growth that I formed a new company and called it Simplicity Circle, which is focused on teaching the simplicity approach to thousands of overwhelmed and frustrated business owners.

Now let's talk about how to apply the simplicity approach to your business so you can grow with confidence, excitement, and ease.

$$\bullet \ \bullet \ \bullet \ \bullet \ \bullet \ \bullet$$

Simplicity Is a Choice

Simple and easy are different. Easy implies little effort.
Simple comes from clarity.
—*Milana Leshinsky*

Most people who talk about simplifying refer to things like leveraging, streamlining, and automating things. All of these can be helpful, but simplifying is more than just taking care of the "symptoms." **It's building simplicity right into the DNA of your business.**

When you choose a growth strategy that's a natural fit for you, your business becomes a full expression of your ideas, dreams, skills, life experiences, and unique personality. That's why it becomes so natural it's almost effortless. It becomes an extension of who you are.

You choose simplicity or complexity with every decision you make – every project you take on, every client you accept, and every strategy you try – and these decisions shape your business and your life. I had a business I loved and a business I dreaded. I can tell you that the business I loved was based on simplicity and total alignment with my natural abilities and personality, and when I did the math I realized that I actually made more money.

You shouldn't have to change to fit your business; your business should change to fit you. It needs to make the most of your unique skills, talents, and view of the world. You'll not only serve the perfect clients for you, you'll show up at your best because your business is in full alignment with who you are. When that happens, everything is incredibly clear and you know exactly what to do to get results. Your business becomes an extension of you, allowing you to make the impact you want and create the lifestyle you desire.

It's time to completely shift your ability and capacity to grow your business, and to start seeing clearly why you've been frustrated or stuck and what you must do next to unleash your business growth.

• • • ● • •

Trapped in Complexity

*People often associate complexity with deeper
meaning, when often after precious time has been lost,
it is realized that simplicity is the key to everything.*
—Gary Hopkins, author, healer

After I left my seven-figure business, I went on
sabbatical. My initial plan was to spend it doing
more travel and writing music, and I did both. But
after a couple of months I was drawn back to business.
Specifically, I wanted to figure out the true nature of
business success and find out:

- *Why some business owners are really successful
  and others are struggling.*
- *Why even successful entrepreneurs find
  themselves unhappy.*

What I found was very exciting and completely different from what I was taught. I had learned that you just had to want it bad enough and push hard enough to get the results you wanted. I had learned that hustling and working hard were the only ways to succeed in business. I like to call this kind of thinking "the cult of the grind."

The cult of the grind puts you to shame for not being willing to put in long hours and sleepless nights and do whatever needs to be done to reach success. There's honor in the grind. People respect your ability and willingness to work tirelessly to achieve results. It's normal and even expected to become a "business warrior" if you want to succeed. This belief is causing massive overwhelm and burnout for many entrepreneurs, and traps you in a game that is impossible to win.

You know you're trapped in complexity if you agree with at least two of the following:

1. I constantly feel busy, tired, or anxious about my business; I'm always "on."
2. My mind is frequently in a state of chaos, overwhelm, and worry about not having enough time to do what needs to be done.

3. Growing a business feels hard and exhausting, like climbing a mountain.
4. I often procrastinate or feel like I'm not really doing what I "should" be doing.
5. My business has hit a plateau and I need to start making more money!
6. I often feel self-doubt and question my business decisions.
7. I feel uninspired and uncreative in regard to my business.
8. I judge myself for playing too small.
9. I often feel FOMO – the "Fear of Missing Out" – when I watch my peers.
10. I'm unclear about the direction of my business, and keep reinventing myself.
11. I have studied many programs and strategies, but I'm still not getting results.

These are just a few signs that you're operating on the complexity mindset. In other words, *you're pushing for results instead of aligning yourself with the right strategy.*

What I discovered during my sabbatical is that it's possible to create a business that allows you to do your best work, focus on what you love, and create massive results without the stress and anxiety that so many business owners experience. It's possible to be paid extremely well for the work you enjoy. Your business can give you freedom instead of trapping you. To do that, however, you need to know what to avoid. So let's take a look at what causes complexity in a growing business.

• • • • • • •

Nine Complexity Traps

There's no guru. You are the guru.
—Milana Leshinsky

Every business starts with an idea – you see some sort of need in the market and feel that you can support it. And make a living along the way. You're excited and you're ready to jump in. You love the dream of creating a business, but before you know it you move away from your core idea, and the creative, inspired entrepreneur who started the business suddenly has to become a leader and manager.

Some people find that that's exactly what they were born to do: lead, manage, and build an empire. But many don't want that at all. Before they know it, they're managing a team, delivering multiple programs and services, and planning their growth strategy for the next five years. Little by little, complexity begins to creep in. The business starts taking over their life, and the lifestyle they were dreaming about goes out the window. Every product launch, every joint venture, every event, and every client brings a new layer of responsibility into their life. Stress and anxiety become the norm.

I've talked to dozens of my peers in the last few months who said that they find themselves in the midst of such complexity that they simply cannot go on. Except they must go on. They have clients and a team to support. They have commitments and obligations.

When I had conversations with business owners who were on the brink of burnout, I identified the nine biggest complexity traps that might be derailing and even crippling your business growth right now. These traps are so powerful, they convince you that there's no other way. They undermine your business growth and make your life much harder than it needs to be. When you escape these traps, you will be able to accelerate your business growth because everything that remains moves you forward simply and easily.

#1: Working with Multiple Brands or Niche Markets

Trying to market your business to different groups of people requires building multiple mailing lists, websites, and lead magnets and developing multiple marketing channels. This usually happens because you don't want to limit how many people you serve. But it actually dilutes the effectiveness of your marketing. You can end up spending a lot of time and effort growing your business, but not necessarily generate more income.

This is why it's so important to have a specific message or philosophy for your business. When you have an exciting and clear message; when you take a powerful stand on a specific topic – I call this a "big idea" – suddenly everything falls into place. You know exactly who to market to, what products and services to create, and where to spend your time to reach your ideal audience.

I'm sure I offered over one hundred different products and programs in the course of my career, but I've always taken a stand for helping coaches, authors, and speakers turn their expertise into lifestyle businesses. I've always known where and how to reach my ideal clients, which gave me the laser focus I needed to thrive despite having no previous business experience.

#2: Juggling Multiple Partners or Promotions

I've used joint ventures throughout my businesses, and I totally love the idea of having JV partners who support each other, promote each other, and build a bigger mailing list. But as I look back at how I was working with my JV partners, I realize this was a big part of what created complexity for me. My calendar was filled with weekly partner promotions. Some weeks I had to support multiple partners, and sometimes those promotions overlapped my own.

I'm not alone in this. I see many of my peers and clients trying to figure out how to promote lots of different products, programs, and partners at the same time, and how to squeeze "just one more promotion" into their calendar! This is how they get themselves into situations that lead to complexity and confusion.

The way to avoid falling into this trap is to be very strategic and have a very clear "unifying strategy" for your business – a single aim that guides all your actions and activities – and use it as a filter for making all your decisions. Just because you can promote someone or something doesn't mean it's the right thing for your business.

#3: Investing in Multiple Training Programs or Multiple Mentors at the Same Time

I recently worked with two different coaches at the same time, and each one literally told me to do what the other said I should never do. I felt confused because I respected both of them. They were both smart and successful business owners, so I found myself paralyzed and unable to move forward in either direction. And I've seen others enroll in multiple training programs and then try to keep up with all of them, which can lead to burnout.

The best way to avoid this complexity trap is to focus on one training, mentor, or system at a time. This is hard to do because you see a new product launch every week and you want to try all the trainings, all the programs, all the new secret methods. But when you get clear on your ideal business model and understand your marketing personality, it's easy to ignore the strategies and programs that are not good fits for you.

#4: Jumping from One System to Another without Understanding Why the First One Didn't Work

How many training or coaching programs have you invested in over the last few years? If you've been trying to grow your business, probably quite a few, right? Some of them worked for you a little, and others didn't do anything at all. When a new program lands in your inbox and it looks attractive, you're probably thinking, "Now *this* one may be the answer to my problem."

We go through training after training, system after system, without any significant results... and we never stop and ask ourselves, "Why didn't I get results?" Sometimes we blame the creator of the program; sometimes we blame ourselves – we're not smart enough, or we weren't ready enough, or we just didn't implement everything.

When you operate on the simplicity approach, you ask yourself this question before investing in any system or program: "Is it going to allow me to leverage and build on my superskills?" Your "superskills" are those natural abilities, aptitudes, and skills that allow you to create results with ease. When you ignore your superskills you end up frustrated, restless, and uninspired. You get stuck all the time yet keep pushing hard to get to the result.

Over the two decades of my business journey, every time I took a leap in my income and made the biggest impact it was because I used my superskills. But many seasoned entrepreneurs have no awareness of their superskills. They work hard, grind away, push and pull, believing that's the only way to succeed and grow.

I've been investing in speaker training for years, but I've never been able to get the kind of results that I see other people get. Today I know that speaking is actually not one of my superskills, which is fine because I have a few others that allow me to get amazing results. In fact, I discovered that I can be a great speaker when I focus on *teaching*. Speakers typically focus on inspiring and motivating their audiences, which doesn't come naturally to me. I had to tweak my approach to speaking before experiencing great results.

You may also choose to delegate the activities and projects that are essential to the success of your business but are not among your superskills. If you don't know what your superskills are, you can struggle for years trying to achieve results from systems and strategies that don't fit you well.

When I left my last business, I knew I was going to start a new one and develop new programs and products. This time I wanted to be sure to honor the unique personalities and natural abilities of my clients. Today I always keep in mind that one size does *not* fit all; that just because I was successful with a strategy doesn't mean my clients will be; and that when I say my system is the fastest and easiest way to achieve business growth, it's because it allows you to leverage your own superskills.

#5: Rapidly Growing a Team to Support Multiple Projects and Goals

Whether you have one virtual assistant or a team of ten, you can still fall into this trap. I used to say, "If you don't want to do something, or don't have the skills, delegate! Outsource!" But when you hire other people you end up creating a team that you must manage! You now have more decisions to make and more challenges are taking up space in your brain. All of this adds a new layer of complexity to your business.

After I learned about organizational charts, I went from having three people on my team to suddenly running a team of twelve in a matter of months. At first it was a great source of pride and accomplishment – I now had a *real* company with a big team! But within a few months I watched my agile, fast-paced business turn into a slow-creeping "train." Discussions and decisions had to go through multiple layers of the team, making every project or idea take forever to come to life. It became a frustrating experience with "complexity" written all over it.

I'm not suggesting that you should not hire a team; you need support to achieve your goals. But you want to hire people to support the right projects at the right times – projects that fit into your *unifying strategy* and help you achieve your most important goals. Hire people only when you see that as the next natural step for you to grow your business.

#6: Constant Comparison to Highly Successful People in the Industry

This trap is actually the underlying hidden reason for the complexity that many people experience. Everyone at every level of income is watching what others are doing and wondering, "Why can't I do that? What's wrong with me? Others are making ten times what I'm making!"

I remember completing a quarter-of-a-million-dollar launch and feeling like I had failed because my friend had just had a two-million-dollar launch. This kind of thinking can lead to a lot of stress and unhappiness. No matter how well you do in your business, it never *feels* good enough because someone else is doing better. You can try to imitate them, but everyone is different; they have different superskills than you do.

Simplicity happens when you're confident in your superskills and you know that nobody else does it like you do. You can get results with much more ease when you're aware of your superskills and build all aspects of your business around them.

#7: The Cult of the Guru

Most business training programs and courses claim to offer a system, a template, a "magic button," a "tested and proven" method. *Just do what it says, and success is inevitable.* The reality is that only a small percentage of people actually succeed with any system, method, or course. That's because they're based on the people who created them. "You want success? I am the prototype. This is the way to do it." They rarely leave room for you to be you. Your natural abilities and skills, your passions and dreams, your lifestyle and experiences – all of these should be considered when deciding how to grow your business.

Simplicity entrepreneurs know that following someone else's "success system" blindly just because they're the "guru" can be a very frustrating and disappointing experience. Before following a system or method, simplicity entrepreneurs ask these questions:

- *Is this the best way to go?*
- *Is this the most ideal way to share my message?*
- *Is this going to bring out my passion?*
- *Does this reinforce my superskills?*
- *Can I keep doing this consistently?*

There are many ways to grow a business. The goal is to grow in the right direction for you. When you choose the wrong growth strategy it takes a huge amount of energy to get anywhere – like climbing a mountain. When you make the right choice for *you*, you feel an immediate sense of relief, confidence, excitement, and clarity.

Simplicity entrepreneurs stretch outside their comfort zone differently from everyone else. They know that learning new skills and strategies allows them to grow to the next level. They simply stretch themselves in the right direction – one of alignment and building on their natural skills and abilities.

#8: Play Big or Go Home

What comes to mind when you think of playing big? To many entrepreneurs, playing big means stepping up and doing whatever it takes to build a multimillion-dollar business: big launches, big events, expensive marketing, getting into media, doing big joint ventures, building a big team. This is a complexity trap because you can find yourself investing a lot more time, effort, and money on managing that.

When simplicity entrepreneurs want to play big, they start by taking a stand for what they believe in – their most important message to the world. They stop following what everyone else is doing and make a decision to create their own business path that fits their personality and life. To them, playing big means waking up every day and having the freedom to do what moves them. And because they do what they love, they end up making a lot more money, too.

It's not about playing big or small; it's about figuring out how to leverage and showcase your greatest skills and abilities to create the kind of business you want and generate the kind of impact you are truly capable of.

#9. FOMO, or Fear of Missing Out

FOMO is a state of anxiety caused by the fear of missing out on something that everyone else is participating in. It makes you click on a link, watch a video, join a frenzy of followers, and buy the product that everyone's been talking about.

We all experience FOMO once in a while. It can come with a feeling of potential loss and cause you to make irrational decisions and buy stuff you don't need. Simplicity entrepreneurs don't experience FOMO as often because they have confidence and clarity around the kind of business they are building. They think about their goals, top values, and what truly matters to them. They ask these questions to make a confident decision:

- *Will this new thing contribute to or take away from my biggest goals and values?*
- *Will it build on my natural abilities?*

- *Will it help me leverage my strengths?*
- *Will it support or distract from my vision for my business and life?*

In other words, they know that anything they add to their business can create complexity, and they filter their buying decisions through the mindset of simplicity entrepreneurship.

Those are the top nine complexity traps I identified. If you're not aware of how they can cripple your growth, your business might consume and take over your life, throwing you off balance in other areas such as health and relationships. A question I often get when I talk about simplicity is "Are you saying that everything should be easy, simple, and effortless in business?" Not quite, so let me explain.

• • • • • • •

Temporary Complexity

If it feels right, I do it. If it doesn't feel right, I don't do it. If I don't know, I wait until I know.
—*Stephanie Bennett Vogt, author of* A Year to Clear

Imagine going to the beach. The sand is soft and warm, the ocean is sparkling in the afternoon sun, and you can't wait to immerse yourself in the clear blue water to feel its gentle warmth on your skin. You've been really anticipating this moment.

But first you have to overcome the initial feeling of cold water until your body gets used to it. You have to push and use your will power to take step after step until you're finally comfortable enough to go all the way in and enjoy the swimming. I call this "temporary complexity."

Real growth happens when you stretch yourself outside your comfort zone. Staying inside your comfort zone keeps you from taking risks, trying new ideas, developing new skills, growing as an entrepreneur, and ultimately achieving the success and financial freedom you've been working towards. So if you use the simplicity approach, does it mean you never get to experience the growth that comes with stretching yourself outside your comfort zone?

Not at all. In fact, in my entrepreneurial career I have consistently pushed myself outside my comfort zone, trying new skills and learning new strategies all the time. I had to learn computer programming, web design, graphic design, copywriting, marketing, selling, video production, event planning, curriculum development, public speaking, training, coaching, project management, joint venture partnerships, networking, webinars, social media, product launches, branding, and many other things required to run a successful business online.

I reached a certain level of competency in all of these. I excelled at just a few – my superskills. These are the skills that allowed me to build multiple six- and seven-figure businesses over the course of two decades without any previous business experience. **No matter how hard I worked on mastering all of these skills, I experienced significant results in just a few of them.**

Imagine if I had known what those superskills were early on...

- *How much time and frustration would I have saved myself?*
- *How much more joy would I have experienced in my entrepreneurial journey?*
- *How much more clarity and confidence would I have felt when faced with overwhelming choices and decisions?*

You absolutely can stretch yourself outside your comfort zone, but while doing so, pay attention to your most natural skills and abilities. For example, I had never led a webinar until 2004. (I had never even heard this term until a year before then.) Twenty-five people attended my first webinar, and one of them purchased my product at the end. I was able to attract one hundred people to my second webinar, twelve of whom signed up for my program.

I had to learn the technology, the content design, the slides creation, and webinar marketing, all of which stretched me outside my comfort zone. Seeing consistent improvement in my results, I continued to work on mastering this strategy, eventually leading to a webinar attended by two thousand people, which resulted in three hundred new customers and half-a-million dollars in sales.

I had to go through the temporary complexity to get to the feeling of joy, confidence, and ease in delivering profitable webinars. At the time I didn't know that designing and leading webinar presentations involved using some of my biggest superskills – *developing, simplifying, and teaching complex frameworks.* All I knew was that I truly enjoyed doing it, I always received amazing feedback from participants, and every time I offered a webinar my sales grew. Had I been aware of this earlier, I would've allowed myself to drop many of the other strategies and skills I was painfully trying to master, such as design and networking, and focus my business growth strategy around the ones that came more naturally to me. I had to stretch outside my comfort zone and learn some new tools and skills, *but this period of temporary complexity allowed me to achieve simplicity in my business.*

But problems occur when the complexity never ends. Imagine walking into the cold ocean water and it just never feels warmer, even after you've been immersed in it for fifteen minutes. When a skill or strategy you've been trying to implement is not based on your superskills, you never warm to it, and you can get trapped for a very long time in the complexity of trying to integrate it into your skillset.

If you're currently trapped in complexity, begin applying the following simplicity entrepreneurship principles and steps to your business.

• • • • • •

How to Become a Simplicity Entrepreneur

The ability to simplify means to eliminate the
unnecessary so that the necessary may speak.
—Hans Hofmann, artist

Here are the eleven steps I recommend for becoming a simplicity entrepreneur:

1. Keep asking yourself these two questions:

    *   *"When am I in the flow?" (You're in the flow*
        when you're enjoying what you're doing and
        results come with more ease than when you're
        involved in other projects and activities.)

    *   *"Where does it feel like I'm pushing too*
        hard?" (You're pushing too hard when your

results don't match your expectations and the amount of effort you put in. When this happens, adjust your activities and decisions based on what feels more fluid.)

2.   Choose one niche and claim it. Focus on it. Take a stand in it. When you do, you'll know exactly who to market to, what message to share, what products and services to create, and where to spend your time to reach your ideal audience. Working with multiple brands, niches, and marketing messages creates lack of focus and diminishes results.

3.   "Unplug" often to create space for your mind to do its magic. Rest is part of work. Every time you leave your office, you come back with new ideas. Best solutions and fresh insights come to you naturally when you're not pushing to find them.

4.   Let go of what others think of your choices and decisions. Stop trying to please other people.

Simplicity happens when you're able to let go of what others tell you to do or to believe. Make business decisions based on what feels right to you.

5. If it feels good, go for it. If it doesn't feel good, don't do it. If you don't know, wait until you know. And get comfortable in the "not knowing."

6. In business there is always too much to try and too much to do. Take a deep breath and know that you can do it all, just not all at once and not all right now.

7. Become aware of your highest natural abilities, your superskills. Then design every area of your business around them.

8. **Your business should be a perfect fit for who you are.** This is the entire premise of simplicity – in order for you to be successful, your business should be a full expression of your personality, skills, and passions.

9. Hire team members only when you know exactly why you need them, what work they'll be performing, and when it's the next obvious step in the growth of your business.

10. Surround yourself with other simplicity entrepreneurs.

11. Make simplicity a core value of your business.

• • • • • • •

SIMPLICITY ENTREPRENEURSHIP MANIFESTO

The only tasks that you will need to continue for the rest of your life are those of choosing what to keep and what to discard and of caring for the things you decide to keep.
—*Marie Kondo, author of* The Life-Changing Magic of Tidying Up

SIMPLICITY ENTREPRENEURS CHOOSE TO THINK AND ACT ACCORDING TO THESE IDEAS:

1. FOCUS ON ESSENTIALS

I choose to "overlook" many opportunities and focus on the few that will make all the difference. I focus on the essentials that truly matter.

2. GROW WITHOUT ADDING

I believe that growth doesn't have to come from adding more products, more strategies, or more team members to my business. It can come from focus and alignment.

3. PROFIT WITHOUT TRADEOFF

I want to make money, make an impact, and create a profitable business, but not *at all costs*. Profitability doesn't have to take away from peace of mind.

4. TRUST MY INNER GURU

I trust my own inner guidance when faced with various options and paths. I ignore the noise and advice that doesn't fit my goals, values, and beliefs.

5. BUILD FOR JOY

I focus on finding the growth strategies that bring me joy. I believe that business is part of life, not the other way around.

• • • • • •

My Invitation to You

What can I go big on?
—Greg McKeown, author of Essentialism

There are many tools out there that help you understand your personality and natural abilities. Most of these, however, leave it at that – without a way to interpret or apply the results to your business in practical ways. In my training I take it a step further and show you how to not only discover what your superskills are, but also how to build them into the *five most important areas of your business* for maximum growth.

If you enjoyed this short book and wonder how *you* can create a highly profitable, simplicity-driven business, I invite you to watch a video I created for you:

• • • • • •

FREE Video:

"Monetize Your Superskills:
Discover Your Unique Path to Profit,
Leverage Your Natural Abilities, and
Grow Your Business with Clarity,
Confidence, and Ease!"

Just go to
www.simplicitycircle.com/superskills
to start watching.

The simplicity approach gives you a clear direction and liberates you from having to do things that don't pay off or that drain your time and energy. You'll also discover why you've been stuck or frustrated, and you'll start seeing a clear and almost obvious path to growth for your business.

ABOUT MILANA LESHINSKY

Milana Leshinsky created a million-dollar coaching and information business empire. She is the creator of "Recurring Revenue Revolution," the author of *Coaching Millions*, the  inventor of *telesummit*, the co-founder of the JV Insider Circle, and the founder of Simplicity Circle, where she takes complexity out of growing a business. Milana came from the Soviet Ukraine in 1992 as a classical musician with zero knowledge of the business world, and built a million-dollar business from home while raising her two children. In her spare time she takes ballroom dance lessons and writes music.

To learn more about Milana's programs and events, read her blog, or explore working with her, visit her website at http://www.SimplicityCircle.com.

Acknowledgments

I would like to acknowledge:

My dear family and friends. I don't think I'd have a purpose in this life without you.

Shawn Driscoll, my business coach who was there for me during a challenging transition. Thank you for holding the space for me to discover the real meaning of simplicity in business.

Christine Kloser, for inspiring me to see simplicity in action. Your events are so masterful and transformational. I feel very fortunate to live close enough to attend them without having to fly.

Madeleine Davis, an unexpected gift who came into my life when I needed to believe in myself again. Your amazing spirit, strategic thinking, and brilliant ideas couldn't have come at a better time!

Tammy Burke, a dear friend who is always there for me. I'm so happy you were back in the area just in time to remind me it was time to leave the hustle and find simplicity again.

Danielle Miller, for helping me come up with a simplicity framework before I knew how to teach it. I love our lunches!

My clients and members – I'm so grateful that you heard my message of simplicity, even before I knew how to communicate it myself.

Corinne Toomey, for being the best personal assistant I ever imagined! Or actually, didn't imagine. Cory, I hope to continue to work and grow together!

Jonathan Fields, whose article on simplicity-driven entrepreneurship validated the direction of my work. I'm so glad I discovered it before deciding that nobody would be interested in simplicity.

The Arthur Murray Dance studio, especially my instructor **Tim Hippert**, for believing that I could learn to dance even at thirty-nine. I hope we'll still be dancing when I'm a hundred and you're ninety!

And all my **peers, former clients, and online friends** who supported me during my transition and followed me from complexity to simplicity. *I can't wait to share this journey with you!*

Made in the USA
Middletown, DE
03 May 2019